ALFIE AND ROSIE
ADVENTURE BUNNIES

The Tale of Acceptance

Author Tanya E. Ma

Alfie and Rosie books pledge to donate 10% of all its profits to the Rosie Yvonne Foundation. The Rosie Yvonne Foundation promotes the use of animal therapy to help young people suffering from depression. It also strives to help many wonderful furry friends find their forever homes.

The funds will be donated to:

Beyond Blue www.beyondblue.org.au
The Rabbit Sanctuary www.rabbitsanctuary.com.au
RSPCA NSW www.rspcansw.org.au

Please find further information at:

www.alfierosieadventurebunniesbooks.com
www.rosieyvonnefoundation.com

In Loving Memory
of Yvonne

"There is no path to happiness: Happiness is the path."

- Buddhist quote

On an autumn evening, Alfie, a little round apricot and white bunny was sitting by the lake and saw himself in the water.

He saw that he had one ear up and one ear down.

He was sad and thought, "I look funny."

Alfie hopped to his mummy.

He asked, "Why do I have one ear up and one ear down? I look funny. I don't look like my sister Rosie who has two ears down. My ears make me sad, and I feel like I don't fit in."

Alfie's mummy said, "Oh little Alfie, why do you feel sad about the way you look? Rosie and I love you exactly how you are! I wish you would accept and love yourself as much we do!"

Alfie hopped over to his sister Rosie, and he saw both of her ears down and wanted to have ears like her.

Rosie said, "Why are you sad, Alfie?"

Alfie said, "Because other bunnies tease me and call me 'airplane ears'."

Alfie asked Rosie, "What makes you so happy?"

Rosie said, "I am happy because mummy loves us!"

Alfie still felt sad but remembered his mummy being happy after she walked the Camino path in Spain.

He thought, "Maybe if I went and walked the Camino path, I will be happy as well."

Alfie said to Rosie, "Let's walk the Camino path!"

Alfie and Rosie packed their bags.

Alfie and Rosie went to the airport and waved goodbye to their mummy and shouted, "We love you, mummy. We will be back soon!"

Their mummy was scared, but she wanted Alfie to accept and love himself just as he is.

Alfie and Rosie landed in Spain and made their way to the start of the Camino path.

They were excited, but Alfie was still sad about his ears.

BUEN CAMINO

As they hopped along the Camino path, they met Benny, a little hippo.

Benny joined Alfie and Rosie, and they then walked the Camino path together.

BUEN CAMINO

Alfie was still sad. He looked at Rosie with her two ears down.

Alfie thought, "Rosie doesn't look funny. She looks very happy. I wish I had two ears down like Rosie. I would be happy too."

Alfie said, "You are a brave little hippo, Benny, to walk here on your own."

Alfie thought he would be happy if he had two ears down like Rosie and wished he was as brave as Benny.

They went along the path till they met Lily, a small hamster who was very fast. Alfie wished he was as fast as Lily. That would make him happy.

As they went along the path they saw red flags and lots of balloons.

"This looks like fun!" said Benny.

Suddenly, Alfie heard a loud noise with his up ear and heard loud thumps with his down ear. He was scared but knew he had to warn his friends.

"Run! Run off the the path!" yelled Alfie.

They ran to the bushes next to the Camino path as the very big bulls ran past.

Lily, Benny, and Rosie gave Alfie a big hug. His one ear up and one ear down heard the bulls coming and saved them all.

Alfie felt a glow of happiness in his chest and thought, "Wow, I am lucky to have one ear up and one ear down!"

At last, Alfie was happy. His one up and one down ears had heard the bulls coming. His special ears had saved them all. It was good to be different.

Alfie, Rosie, Benny, and Lilly all reached the end of the Camino path.

Alfie realised that he was happy about his ears but also happy that he had made such great friends and had Rosie and mummy in his life whom he loved very much.

He couldn't wait to hug his mummy and tell her how happy he feels now just the way he is.

Alfie looked at Rosie and said, "I think I'm ready to go home. I am happy with who I am now!"

Alfie and Rosie came home and ran up to their mummy. Their mummy scooped Alfie up and gave him a huge kiss. She was so happy to see that Alfie finally accepted and loved himself as much as she did!

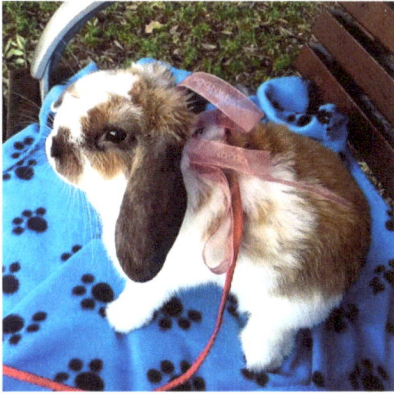

About the Author

Hello, my name is Tanya and I wish to thank you for reading Alfie and Rosie's first book. Alfie and Rosie are my precious furbabies who have brought so much happiness to my life. Therefore, I wished to share their personality and love with the world as well.

I, myself, have walked the long Camino de Santiago pilgrimage which was along the north of Spain for 980 kilometers. On this path, I met many lovely people of different backgrounds, cultures and passions. I learnt a lot of lessons on this path and from the people I met as well.

I wished to write this book and the following books in the Alfie and Rosie Adventure Bunnies' series to promote kindness to animals and create awareness of their wonderful nature and intelligence to children. Also for these books to show the delightful travel adventures that we are fortunate to experience here on earth. Furthermore, as children grow up, they experience many difficult periods, which I hope these books can help them along with.

Owning this book means you have donated and helped people with depression through Beyond Blue as well as animals to be rehomed and rehabilitated via the RSPCA NSW and The Rabbit Sanctuary. So I thank you from the bottom of my heart for this and hope you feel proud that you have helped these charities as well.

Many thanks,

Tanya

My inspiration for this book: The Camino de Santiago

This book is based on my experience of walking the Camino de Santiago where I learned to accept myself for who I am. I am so happy and grateful for my time spent on the Camino because the experience changed me and has helped me in many ways.

The Camino de Santiago is known as the Way of Saint James which is a historical long route in Spain and is an important symbol of the culture and heritage of Europe. Many people walk the Camino for their own reasons and along the Camino you follow the yellow signs that lead you to the destination.

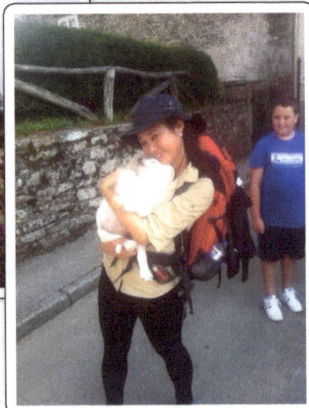

When I walked the Camino, I met many wonderful people with different backgrounds, experiences and strengths whom also became my close friends. We loved discovering the cities in Spain, were in awe of the stunning landscape and treasured the joyful culture that surrounded us.

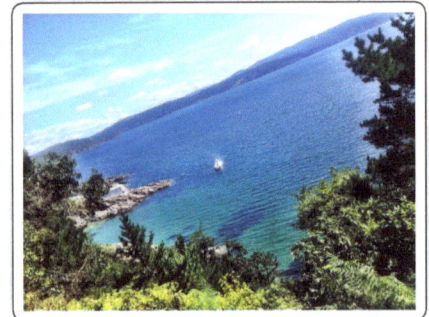

So I hope you have enjoyed experiencing the Camino through this book!